A CAROUSEL OF ANIMALS

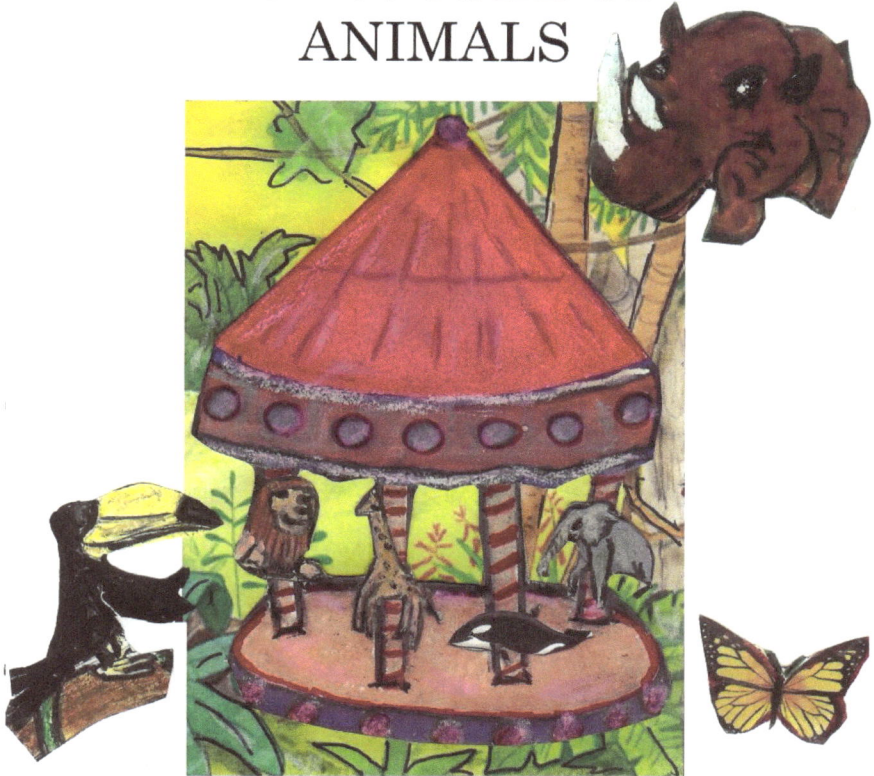

Funny Facts About Animals from A to Z in Verse

By Joyce Spier

DEDICATION

This book is dedicated to Susan, John and Ira Spier for graciously helping me publish this book.

The Anteater

Anteaters are a funny bunch.
It's ants they always seem to munch.
They have unusual tastes in food.
I think their choices very crude.
They sniff for bugs with a great long snout.
Their nose and tongue will scoop them out.
They can eat a ton of bugs.
They devour termites, ants and grubs.
I'm glad that my foods still exist.
If I'm served ants, I shall resist.

The Butterfly

A Butterfly starts as a wormy thing.
It forms a cocoon I've been told.
It emerges early in the spring.
It's a wonderful sight to behold.
I wish, when I get old and blue,
I'd sleep in a cocoon like shell.
And when I awoke, I had morphed into
A person young and well.

The Camel

The Camel has a funny bump.
It's on his back. It's called a hump.
If you should ride one, then you'll know
How fast a camel can really go.
He hardly drinks, a wonderful feature!
It's perfect for a desert creature.

The Donkey

The Donkey is a cousin to a horse.
He's used for transporting and riding, of course.
He works very hard and can follow an order.
He's called a burro south of the border.
Donkeys are stubborn in Loony Toons.
HE-HA to all those silly cartoons.

The Elephant

"I have a versatile trunk.
It helps me get water and food.
I can cart away garbage and junk.
When I get in a jovial mood.
I've pals in India and Africa too.
But my ivory's safe when I'm in a zoo."

The Flamingo

Oh how wondrous is the Flamingo!
You may see one in Santo Domingo.
It has long pink legs with big webbed feet.
And a neck that bends to help it eat.
We will all stop and stare,
When those pretty pink wings take to the air.

The Giraffe

His neck goes up a great long way.
Up to the leaves of the trees.
He eats pounds and pounds of leaves each day,
And can fight off a lion with great ease.
His coat has brown spots over golden tan.
He's the tallest creature in animal land.

The Hippo

"I'm a Hippo who likes to dip-o
In jungle water and mud.
You can call me ugly.
But I can say smugly
That Hippo girls think I'm a stud."

The Iguana

"I am an Iguana.
And I can be your pet.
Central America was
My first habitat.
Keep my cage warm,
To keep me alive,
Feed me fresh greens
To see that I thrive.
My scaled reptile body is a dull brownish
green.
But my tail is the longest that you've ever
seen."

The Jackal

The Jackal hunts just like a bully.
He chases small things so willy-nilly.
He always catches what he needs.
Big strong feet provide his great speeds.
"Jackals live in families," said a good
source.
I don't know a Jackal who filed for divorce.

The Kangaroo

This Australian animal's a marsupial,
With a gait that's unusually unusual.
This creature has a pouch you know.
Where babies eat and sleep and grow.
His forearms are short, with plenty of
clout.
The tail forms a third leg to hop-stop about.
Be careful around him. He's a good boxer
too.
He has a lead role in Winnie the Pooh.

The Lion

My name is Howard. And I'm no coward.
Time will remember that.
Now don't be a wussy. I'm only a pussy
Who lives at the zoo and gets fat.
My species declining, while I'm here reclining.
I feel really bad about that.
So try to protect us and make grasslands precious
For my cousins to wander about.

The Mouse

"I'm just a Mouse and it's a mistake
When people see me and scream and shake.
I'm not a rat, just a field mouse.
Forget the trap! Don't be a louse.
Think of the mice you think so grand.
The ones who reign over Disneyland."

The Newt

A Newt is like a salamander.
It mostly lives on land.
It must breed in the water.
And lay eggs on wet, wet sand.
A newt is an amphibian.
Some have lungs and gills.
You will never ever find them.
Where they may get the chills.

The Octopus

Octopi live in the salty sea.
They have eight sinewy arms to use.
If those arms were legs, how regretfully,
They would feel buying four pair of shoes.
Some are big. Some small.
They don't have time to think.
If something frightens them at all,
They spew a spray of ink.

The Panda

A Panda is like a black and white bear
That lives where the bamboo grow.
Pandas are extremely rare,
Fur black as ink, and white as snow.
Perhaps China will lend us a few,
So we can see them at a zoo.

The Quail

The Quail is a plump game bird.
To hunt it's considered a sport.
To shoot down a bird is quite absurd,
But hunters don't give that a thought.
They aim their guns from night till dawn.
I'll be glad when hunting's season's gone.

The Rhinoceros

Never tease a Rhinoceros!
To do so would be preposterous.
He'd snort and stomp and stare side to
side,
And show us his horns with obvious pride.
But we can say, "Boo!" to a Rhinoceros.
If the zoo has barrier in front of us.

The Snake

The reptiles that scare me the most are Snakes.
They come in assorted sizes and shapes.
Some live in the desert. Some live where it's wet.
I know a person who keeps one as a pet.

Snakes are cold blooded and to survive,
Are always looking for some place to hide.
They hide from the heat. They hide from the cold.
With body heat normal, they live to grow old.

If you don't bother them, they won't bother you.
Indiana Jones was afraid of them too.

The Toucan

The Toucan is an ugly bird.
He has a generous beak.
Be careful what you say to him,
He can imitate and speak.
He really is a jungle bird,
But he can be a pet.
Just keep his birdcage dry and warm,
And you'll be completely set.

The Unicorn

The Unicorn looks like a one horned horse.
But he's really just a myth.
He appears on ancient tapestries.
But he never did exist.
So just go try and look for him.
He's nowhere to be seen,
Expect in many story books
And all the art museums.

The Vulture

The Vulture is a scavenging bird.
It eats dead creatures, I have heard.
If he is this sort of feeder,
He's an environmental vacuum cleaner.
His stance is very, very regal.
He is related to an eagle.

The Wolf

I saw a Wolf at the zoo one day.
If he could talk, here's what he'd say.
"It makes me really very sad
That fairy tales make Wolves look bad.
People killed us without thinking,
That our populace was shrinking.
The dog and the Wolf are related.
But we were never domesticated."

Xiphactinus Audax

"I was a prehistoric animal.
I was huge and game.
I looked simply dreadful,
And I couldn't pronounce my name,
I swam around the ocean.
For a big fish, I moved fast.
I ate anything in motion.
Aren't you glad I didn't last?"

The Yak

The Yak is a Himalayan cow,
Who lives on mountains
And I know how.
He has a big heart and big lungs
You see.
So he can breathe thin air most easily.
He provides excellent milk and meat.
So the people of Tibet have food to eat.

The Zebra

The Zebra reminds me of a strange kind of horse.
Who has black stripes on his body (of course).
But others say this fact is not right.
His body is black. The stripes are white.
This contradiction caused people to ponder.
But either way, he's an animal wonder.

There is one animal that I have missed,
That wasn't on our content list.
He became the leader of the game,
By using his well developed brain.
He learned to fly without any wings,
And built so many wondrous things.
He mastered the seas and the mountain ranges.
But he better make some changes.
Unless he cleans the planet up,
Global warming will never stop.
And in a million years or two.
They'll be no animals left to view.
Can you guess? I know you can.

The name of this animal is MAN.

www.ingramcontent.com/pod-product-compliance
Lightning Source LLC
Chambersburg PA
CBHW040347060426
42445CB00029B/27